Jesus Called St. Faustina and St. Teresa of Calcutta to Share His Thirst for Souls

by Rev. George W. Kosicki, CSB

MARIAN PRESS
STOCKBRIDGE   MA 01263

PRO CHRISTO ET ECCLESIA

2021

Available from:

Marian Helpers Center
Stockbridge, MA 01263

Prayerline:1-800-804-3823
TheDivineMercy.org
Orderline:1-800-462-7426
ShopMercy.org

Copy Editor:
David Came

Proofreading:
Stephen LaChance and Mary Ellen McDonald

Typesetting:
Mary Ellen McDonald

Cover Design:
William Sosa

Cover photo of St. Faustina, copyright © Marians of the Immaculate Conception, courtesy of Marian Archives; photo of Mother Teresa, copyright © Michael Collopy, used with permission.

For texts from the English Edition of
Diary of Saint Maria Faustina

NIHIL OBSTAT:
†George H. Pearce, SM
Former Archbishop of Suva, Fiji

IMPRIMATUR:
†Joseph F. Maguire
Bishop of Springfield, MA
April 9, 1984

ISBN: 978-0-944203-50-7

Printed in the United States of America by Marian Press

I Thirst

Table of Contents

Preface

Do you thirst like Jesus for the salvation of souls? Do you understand that our Lord thirsted on the Cross for the salvation of every human soul that He created, has created, and will create?

Sharing this "thirst" of Jesus for souls defines, in a sense, the mission and spirituality of both St. Maria Faustina and St. Teresa of Calcutta. Both of them sought to satisfy this thirst of the Lord — whether it was expressed through deep interior suffering for sinners in a convent or by caring for the poorest of the poor on the streets of Calcutta. Perhaps this spirituality can be summed up best when we make "God and Souls" our aim in life, as the thirst of Jesus becomes our own.

In *I Thirst*, Fr. George Kosicki, CSB, develops this powerful theme by drawing upon the writings of both of these saintly women. In the words of St. Teresa of Calcutta, St. Faustina, and our Lord, Fr. Kosicki shows us how understanding Jesus' thirst can revolutionize our ministry to those who are suffering, especially the dying. Further, he helps us discover the connection between our suffering and God's transforming love. We begin to glimpse how that connection can lead us to lasting joy.

If you have been touched by the life and spirituality of these two holy women, *I Thirst* is a booklet you will want to read and re-read over a lifetime of making "God and Souls" your personal motto.

David Came
Former Executive Editor
Marian Press

Chapter One

I Thirst — Satisfying the Thirst of Jesus for Souls

†

Both St. Teresa of Calcutta and St. Faustina heard the cry of Jesus on the Cross: "I thirst" (Jn 19:28). Jesus asked both of them to help satisfy His thirst for souls.

God and Souls in the Life of St. Teresa of Calcutta

In his tribute to Mother Teresa on the occasion of her death, St. John Paul II described the key to Mother Teresa's mission and inspiration in the words of Jesus on the Cross: "I thirst."

Missionary of Charity: this is what Mother Teresa was in name and in fact, offering such an appealing example that she attracted to herself many people who were ready to leave everything to follow Christ present in the poor.

Her mission began every day, before dawn, in the presence of the Eucharist. In the silence of contemplation, Mother Teresa of Calcutta heard the echo of Jesus' cry on the Cross: **I thirst**. This cry, received in the depths of her heart, spurred her to seek out

Jesus in the poor, the abandoned, and the dying on the streets of Calcutta and to all the ends of the earth.

From John Paul II's Sunday *Angelus*, Sept. 7, 1997

Mother Teresa experienced a specific moment of life-changing grace:

> 1946: On the night of September 10, while riding on a train to the mountain town of Darjeeling to recover from suspected tuberculosis, she received her "vocation within a vocation," a calling to serve Him among the poorest of the poor. She would later say: "I abandoned myself totally to God, and He guided me."

Inside the Vatican, October 1997

At various times, St. Teresa of Calcutta referred to this moment of grace and spoke of the word of the dying Jesus, **I thirst**, as the thirst of Jesus for souls. **I thirst** is written on the wall of every chapel of the Missionaries of Charity around the world. In Mother Teresa's letter to her community, she wrote:

> Why does Jesus say **I thirst**? What does it mean? Something so hard to explain in words — if you remember anything from Mother's letter, remember this — **I thirst** is something *much deeper* than Jesus just

saying "I love you." Until you know deep inside that Jesus thirsts for you — you can't begin to know who He wants to be for you. Or who He wants you to be for Him.

The heart and soul of MC [Missionaries of Charity] is only this — the thirst of Jesus' Heart, hidden in the poor. This is the source of every part of MC life. It gives us our *Aim,* our 4th vow, the Spirit of our Society. Satiating the living Jesus in our midst is the Society's only purpose for existing. Can we each say the same for ourselves — that it is our only reason for living? Ask yourself — would it make any difference in my vocation, in my relation to Jesus, in my work, if Jesus' thirst were no longer our *Aim* — no longer on the chapel wall? Would anything change in my life? Would I feel any loss? Ask yourself honestly, and let this be a test for each to see if His thirst is a reality, something alive — not just an idea.

I thirst and **You did it to Me** — Remember always to connect the two, the means with the *Aim.* What God has joined together let no one split apart. Do not underestimate our practical means — the work for the poor, no matter how small or humble — that make our life something beautiful for God. They are the most precious gifts of God to our Society — Jesus' hidden presence so near, so able to touch. Without the work for the poor the *Aim* dies — Jesus' thirst is only words with no meaning, no answer. Uniting the two, our MC vocation will remain alive and real, what Our Lady asked.

Mother Teresa, March 25, 1993

God and Souls in the Life of St. Faustina

In March of 1937 [Holy Week], St. Faustina had a vision of the crucified Lord and heard the words of Jesus, **I thirst**. This moment is a startling parallel to the moment of grace that St. Teresa of Calcutta experienced on the train to Darjeeling, September 10, 1946:

> During Holy Mass, I saw the Lord Jesus nailed upon the cross amidst great torments. A soft moan issued from His Heart. After some time, He said: **I thirst. I thirst for the salvation of souls. Help Me, My daughter, to save souls. Join your sufferings to My Passion and offer them to the heavenly Father for sinners** (*Diary of Saint Maria Faustina Kowalska,* 1032. Also see *Diary,* 583 and 648).

The mission and spirituality of the Missionaries of Charity which began with the moment of special grace in the heart of Mother Teresa on the train,

September 10, 1946, has led over 4,000 missionaries to respond to the cry of Jesus on the Cross: **I thirst, I thirst for souls**. Saint Faustina responded to the same call of Christ's thirst for souls and recorded her call and her response — a challenge to all of us to give all to "God and Souls."

Saint Faustina records this theme of her life, "God and Souls," a number of times in her *Diary*. Right at the beginning of her first notebook, she writes "God and Souls" twice (*Diary*, 3, 5); then at the beginning of the second notebook (*Diary*, 523); and twice more at the beginning of her third notebook (*Diary*, 1003, 1005). This theme significantly introduces her oblation of herself for souls, especially sinners (*Diary*, 309). She gave her all for "God and Souls" (*Diary*, 46, 450, 1062).

She knew that her sanctity was essential to be useful for the Church, so she desired to be a saint and strove for it so that she could save many, many souls. "God and Souls" were her very life.

In 1934, on Holy Thursday, Jesus asked St. Faustina to offer herself for souls:

Holy Thursday. Jesus said to me: **I desire that you make an offering of yourself for sinners and especially for those souls who have lost hope in God's mercy** (*Diary*, 308).

God and Souls — An Act of Oblation

Saint Faustina responded to the Lord's desire with a generous offering of herself and all her sufferings and consolation for the conversion of sinners:

Before heaven and earth, before all the choirs of Angels, before the Most Holy Virgin Mary, before all the Powers of heaven, I declare to the One Triune God that today, in union with Jesus Christ, Redeemer of souls, I make a voluntary offering of myself for the conversion of sinners, especially for those souls who have lost hope in God's mercy. This offering consists in my accepting, with total subjection to God's will, all the sufferings, fears, and terrors with which sinners are filled. In return, I give them all the consolations which my soul receives from my communion with God. In a word, I offer everything for them: Holy Masses, Holy Communions, penances, mortifications, prayers. I do not fear the blows, blows of divine justice, because I am united with Jesus. O my God, in this way I want to make amends to You for the souls that do not trust in Your goodness. I hope against all hope in the ocean of Your mercy. My Lord and my God, my portion — my portion forever, I do not base this act of oblation on my own strength, but on the strength that flows from the merits of Jesus Christ. I will daily repeat this act of self-oblation by pronouncing the following prayer which You Yourself have taught me, Jesus:

O Blood and Water which gushed forth from the Heart of Jesus as a Fount of Mercy for us, I trust in You! (*Diary*, 309).

Saint Maria Faustina of the Most Blessed Sacrament
Holy Thursday, during Holy Mass, March 29, 1934.

God and Souls in Our Lives

Each of the elements of the Divine Mercy message and devotion is for souls, souls, souls, especially sinners and the dying. It is God's thirst and desire, and it became St. Faustina's. She entered into the Lord's thirst and longing for souls. She entered into the pain that the loss of souls and distrust brings our Lord. The very purpose of the elements of the Divine Mercy message and devotion — the Image, the Feast, the Chaplet, the Novena, the 3 o'clock Hour of Mercy — are all for souls, souls, souls.

Lord! What do you want of me? What can I do, or not do, in order to save souls — to fulfill Your thirst and desire for souls? Lord, help me, teach me, guide me. This is Your work.

From within my heart (the author's) come the words: "Offer all for souls! Do not analyze, just offer and rejoice with thanksgiving. Do not analyze. Do not judge. Do not be anxious. Be at peace! Pray without ceasing, rejoice always, in all things give thanks." And later, another word: "Offer all — everything — in union with My Passion, to the Father for souls. Bless all the souls that enter your heart and mind. Bless always even as I bless always."

Saint Faustina, pray for me and all apostles of Divine Mercy. Saint Teresa of Calcutta, help us all by your prayers.

Thirst and Desire for Souls

In the following sections, key texts from the *Diary of Saint Maria Faustina Kowalska* are presented. There are hundreds of other texts on this theme, but these samples are presented to deepen your understanding of the desire of the Lord for souls.

Christ's Thirst for Souls

During Holy Mass, I saw the Lord Jesus nailed upon the cross amidst great torments. A soft moan issued from His Heart. After some time, He said: **I thirst. I thirst for the salvation of souls. Help Me, My daughter, to save souls. Join your sufferings to My Passion and offer them to the heavenly Father for sinners** (*Diary*, 1032).

And later, in the *Diary*:

Today, in the course of a long conversation, the Lord said to me: **How very much I desire the salvation of souls! My dearest secretary, write that I want to pour out My divine life into human souls and sanctify them, if only they were willing to accept My grace. The greatest sinners would achieve great sanctity, if only they would trust in My mercy. The very inner depths of My being are filled to overflowing with mercy, and it is being poured out upon all I have created. My delight is to act in a human soul and to fill it with My mercy and to justify it. My kingdom on earth is My life in the human soul. Write, My secretary, that I Myself am the spiritual guide of souls — and I guide them indirectly through the priest, and lead each one to sanctity by a road known to Me alone** (*Diary*, 1784).

Christ expressed His desire and thirst for souls in various ways.

Christ Thirsts — Especially for Poor Sinners

[Let] the greatest sinners place their trust in My mercy. They have the right before others to trust in the abyss of My

mercy. My daughter, write about My mercy towards tormented souls. Souls that make an appeal to My mercy delight Me. To such souls I grant even more graces than they ask. I cannot punish even the greatest sinner if he makes an appeal to My compassion, but on the contrary, I justify him in My unfathomable and inscrutable mercy. Write: Before I come as a just Judge, I first open wide the door of My mercy. He who refuses to pass through the door of My mercy must pass through the door of My justice ... (*Diary*, 1146).

Christ Asks for Help to Save Souls

Today, I saw the suffering Lord Jesus. He leaned down toward me and whispered softly: **My daughter, help Me to save sinners.** Suddenly, a burning desire to save souls entered my soul. When I recovered my senses, I knew just how I was to help souls, and I prepared myself for greater sufferings (*Diary*, 1645).

Christ Wants to Save All Souls

Today during adoration, the Lord gave me to know how much He desires a soul to distinguish itself by deeds of love. And in spirit I saw how many souls are calling out to us, "Give us God." And the blood of the Apostles boiled up within me. I will not be stingy with it; I will shed it all to the last drop for immortal souls. Although perhaps God will not demand that in the physical sense, in spirit it is possible and no less meritorious (*Diary*, 1249).

Christ Suffers Over Distrust

... **The flames of mercy are burning Me. I desire to pour them out upon human souls. Oh, what pain they cause Me when they do not want to accept them!** ... (*Diary*, 1074).

Christ Suffers Over Offenses

... **Souls without love and without devotion, souls full of egoism and self-love, souls full of pride and arrogance, souls full of deceit and hypocrisy, luke-warm souls who have just enough warmth to keep them alive: My Heart cannot bear this** ... (*Diary*, 1702).

Christ Suffers Over Ingratitude

... **My Heart overflows with great mercy for souls, and especially for poor sinners. If only they could understand that I am the best of Fathers to them and that it is for them that the Blood and**

Water flowed from My Heart as from a fount overflowing with mercy. For them I dwell in the tabernacle as King of Mercy. I desire to bestow My graces upon souls, but they do not want to accept them. You, at least, come to Me as often as possible and take these graces they do not want to accept. In this way you will console My Heart. Oh, how indifferent are souls to so much goodness, to so many proofs of love! My Heart drinks only of the ingratitude and forgetfulness of souls living in the world. They have time for everything, but they have no time to come to Me for graces (*Diary*, 367).

Christ Suffers Over Souls

... Jesus was suddenly standing before me, stripped of His clothes, His body completely covered with wounds, His eyes flooded with tears and blood, His face disfigured and covered with spittle. ... **See what love of human souls has done to Me** ... (*Diary*, 268).

Christ Suffers Over Loss of Souls

On a certain occasion, the Lord said to me, **I am more deeply wounded by the small imperfections of chosen souls than by the sins of those living in the world.** It made me very sad that chosen souls make Jesus suffer, and Jesus told me: **These little imperfections are not all. I will reveal to you a secret of My Heart: what I suffer from chosen souls. Ingratitude in return for so many graces is My Heart's constant food, on the part of [such] a chosen soul. Their love is lukewarm, and My Heart cannot bear it; these souls force Me to reject them. Others distrust My goodness and have no desire to experience that sweet intimacy in their own hearts, but go in search of Me, off in the distance, and do not find Me. This distrust of My goodness hurts Me very much. If My death has not convinced you of My love, what will? Often a soul wounds Me mortally, and then no one can comfort Me. They use My graces to offend Me. There are souls who despise My graces as well as all the proofs of My love. They do not wish to hear My call, but proceed into the abyss of hell. The loss of these souls plunges Me into deadly sorrow. God though I am, I cannot help such a soul because it scorns Me; having a free will, it can spurn Me or love Me. You, who are the dispenser of My mercy, tell all the world about My goodness, and thus you will comfort My Heart** (*Diary*, 580).

Christ Suffers Over Consecrated Souls

Why are You sad today, Jesus? Tell me, who is the cause of Your sadness? And Jesus answered me: **Chosen souls who do not have My spirit, who live according to the letter** [see 2 Cor. 3:6] **and have placed the letter above My spirit, above the spirit of love** (*Diary*, 1478).

Christ Delights in Souls with Living Faith

When I steeped myself in prayer, I was transported in spirit to the chapel, where I saw the Lord Jesus, exposed in the monstrance. In place of the monstrance, I saw the glorious face of the Lord, and He said to me: **What you see in reality, these souls see through faith. Oh, how pleasing to Me is their great faith! You see, although there appears to be no trace of life in Me, in reality it is present in its fullness in each and every Host. But for Me to be able to act upon a soul, the soul must have faith. O how pleasing to Me is living faith!** (*Diary*, 1420).

Christ Delights in Souls Who Trust

Let souls who are striving for perfection particularly adore My mercy, because the abundance of graces which I grant

them flows from My mercy. I desire that these souls distinguish themselves by boundless trust in My mercy. I Myself will attend to the sanctification of such souls. I will provide them with everything they will need to attain sanctity. The graces of My mercy are drawn by means of one vessel only, and that is — trust. The more a soul trusts, the more it will receive. Souls that trust boundlessly are a great comfort to Me, because I pour all the treasures of My graces into them. I rejoice that they ask for much, because it is My desire to give much, very much. On the other hand, I am sad when souls ask for little, when they narrow their hearts (*Diary*, 1578).

Christ Loves Souls

I desire that priests proclaim this great mercy of Mine towards souls of sinners. Let the sinner not be afraid to approach Me. The flames of mercy are burning Me — clamoring to be spent; I want to pour them out upon these souls (*Diary*, 50).

Christ Desires the Sanctity of Souls

... O my Jesus, I know that, in order to be useful to souls, one has to strive for the closest possible union with You, who are

Eternal Love. One word from a soul united to God effects more good in souls than eloquent discussions and sermons from an imperfect soul (*Diary*, 1595).

Christ is Merciful Toward Souls

Holy Trinity, One God, incomprehensible in the greatness of Your mercy for creatures, and especially for poor sinners, You have made known the abyss of Your mercy, incomprehensible and unfathomable [as it is] to any mind, whether of man or angel. Our nothingness and our misery are drowned in Your greatness. O Infinite Goodness, who can ever praise You sufficiently? Can there be found a soul that understands You in Your love? O Jesus, there are such souls, but they are few (*Diary*, 361).

Saint Faustina's Thirst for Souls

Saint Faustina took Christ's thirst for souls as her own, and this thirst was reflected (as it was in Mother Teresa) in all her desires, prayers, and actions.

Low Sunday: Today, I again offered myself to the Lord as a holocaust for sinners. My Jesus, if the end of my life is already approaching, I beg You most humbly, accept my death in union with You as a holocaust which I offer You today, while I still have full possession of my faculties and a fully conscious will, and this for a threefold purpose:

Firstly: that the work of Your mercy may spread throughout the whole world and that the Feast of The Divine Mercy may be solemnly promulgated and celebrated.

Secondly: that sinners, especially dying sinners, may have recourse to Your mercy and experience the unspeakable effects of this mercy.

Thirdly: that all the work of Your mercy may be realized according to Your wishes, and for a certain person who is in charge of this work ... .

Accept, most merciful Jesus, this, my inadequate sacrifice, which I offer to You today before heaven and earth. May Your Most Sacred Heart, so full of mercy, complete what is lacking in my offering, and offer it to Your Father for the conversion of sinners. I thirst after souls, O Christ (*Diary,* 1680).

This thirst was expressed by St. Faustina in a variety of ways:

Saint Faustina Desired Souls

O God, how I desire that souls come to know You and to see that You have created them because of Your unfathomable love. O My Creator and Lord, I feel that I am going to remove the veil of heaven so that earth will not doubt Your goodness ... (*Diary*, 483).

Saint Faustina Asked for Souls — Especially Sinners

O Jesus, how sorry I feel for poor sinners. Jesus, grant them contrition and repentance. Remember Your own sorrowful Passion. I know Your infinite mercy and cannot bear it that a soul that has cost You so much should perish. Jesus, give me the souls of sinners; let Your mercy rest upon them. Take everything away from me, but give me souls. I want to become a sacrificial host for sinners. Let the shell of my body conceal my offering, for Your Most Sacred Heart is also hidden in a Host, and certainly You are a living sacrifice ... (*Diary*, 908).

Saint Faustina Encouraged Trust in God's Mercy

... I want to tell souls of Your goodness and encourage them to trust in Your mercy. That is my mission, which You Yourself have entrusted to me, O Lord, in this life and in the life to come (*Diary*, 1325).

Saint Faustina Prayed for the Conversion of Sinners

Before heaven and earth, before all the choirs of Angels, before the Most Holy Virgin Mary, before all the Powers of heaven, I declare to the One Triune God that today, in union with Jesus Christ, Redeemer of souls, I make a voluntary offering of myself for the conversion of sinners, especially for those souls who have lost hope in God's mercy. This offering consists in my accepting, with total subjection to God's will, all the sufferings, fears, and terrors with which sinners are filled. In return, I give them all the consolations which my soul receives from my communion with God. In a word, I offer everything for them: Holy Masses, Holy Communions, penances, mortifications, prayers (*Diary*, 309).

Saint Faustina Asked for Mercy — Especially for Sinners

On these two days, I received Holy Communion as an act of reparation, and I said to the Lord, "Jesus, I offer everything today for sinners. Let the blows of Your justice fall on me, and the sea of Your mercy engulf the poor sinners" (*Diary*, 927).

Saint Faustina Atoned for Sinners

... Jesus, give me the souls of sinners; let Your mercy rest upon them. Take everything away from me, but give me souls. I want to become a sacrificial host for sinners ... (*Diary*, 908).

Saint Faustina Offered All for Souls

At the beginning of Lent, I also asked to have the subject of my particular examen changed, and I was told to do everything with the pure intention of reparation for poor sinners. This keeps me in continual union with God, and this intention perfects my actions, because everything I do is done for immortal souls. All hardships and fatigue are as nothing when I think that they reconcile sinful souls with God (*Diary*, 619).

Saint Faustina Lived for Souls

I know that I live, not for myself, but for a great number of souls. I know that graces granted me are not for me alone, but for souls. O Jesus, the abyss of Your mercy has been poured into my soul, which is an abyss of misery itself. Thank You, Jesus, for the graces and the pieces of the Cross which You give me at each moment of my life (*Diary*, 382).

Saint Faustina Did Penance for Souls

When we left the doctor's [office] and stepped into the sanatorium chapel for a moment, I heard these words in my soul: **My child, just a few more drops in your chalice; it won't be long now.** Joy filled my soul; this was the first call from my beloved Spouse and Master. My heart melted, and there was a moment when my soul was immersed in the whole sea of God's mercy. I felt that my mission was beginning in all its fullness. Death destroys nothing that is good. I pray most of all for souls that are experiencing inner sufferings ... (*Diary*, 694).

Saint Faustina Suffered for Souls

... I united my sufferings with the sufferings of Jesus and offered them for myself and for the conversion of souls who do not trust in the goodness of God ... (*Diary*, 323).

Saint Faustina Prayed for Souls

... I offered the whole day for dying sinners. ... After Holy Communion, I turned my gaze with trust toward the Lord and told Him, "Jesus, I so much desire to tell You something." And the Lord looked at me with love and said: **And what is it that you desire to tell Me?**

"Jesus, I beg You, by the inconceivable power of Your mercy, that all the souls who will die today escape the fire of hell, even if they have been the greatest sinners ... " (*Diary*, 873).

Saint Faustina United Herself With the Passion and Blood of Christ

... O Jesus, be mindful of Your own bitter Passion and do not permit the loss of souls redeemed at so dear a price of Your most precious Blood. O Jesus, when I consider the great price of Your Blood, I rejoice at its immensity, for one drop alone would have been enough for the salvation of all sinners. Although sin is an abyss of wickedness and ingratitude, the price paid for us can never be equalled. Therefore, let every soul trust in the Passion of the Lord, and place its hope in His mercy ... (*Diary*, 72).

Saint Faustina Offered Herself as a Host

... O Jesus, outwardly I want to be hidden, just like this little wafer wherein the eye perceives nothing, and yet I am a host consecrated to You (*Diary*, 641).

Saint Faustina Strove for Sanctity

I strive for the greatest perfection possible in order to be useful to the Church.

Greater by far is my bond to the Church. The sanctity or the fall of each individual soul has an effect upon the whole Church ... (*Diary*, 1475).

Saint Faustina Prayed for Priests and Religious

... I am suffering as much as my weak nature can bear, all for immortal souls, to plead the mercy of God for poor sinners and to beg for strength for priests. Oh, how much reverence I have for priests; and I am asking Jesus, the High Priest, to grant them many graces (*Diary*, 953).

Saint Faustina Prayed for Grace for Souls

... I saw the Mother of God with the Infant in her arms. And a moment later, the Infant Jesus disappeared from the arms of His Mother, and I saw the living image of Jesus Crucified. The Mother of God told me to do what she had done, that, even when joyful, I should always keep my eyes fixed on the Cross, and she told me that the graces God was granting me were not for me alone, but for other souls as well (*Diary*, 561).

Saint Faustina Prayed for the Dying

When I immersed myself in prayer and united myself with all the Masses that were being celebrated all over the world at that time, I implored God, for the sake of all these Holy Masses, to have mercy on the world and especially on poor sinners who were dying at that moment. At the same instant, I received an interior answer from God that a thousand souls had received grace through the prayerful mediation I had offered to God. We do not know the number of souls that is ours to save through our prayers and sacrifices; therefore, let us always pray for sinners (*Diary,* 1783).

Saint Faustina Sought to be Useful to the Church

I am striving for sanctity, because in this way I shall be useful to the Church. I make constant efforts in practicing virtue. I try faithfully to follow Jesus ... (*Diary*, 1505).

Saint Faustina Drew Down Satan's Hate for Mercy and Herself

Satan has admitted to me that I am the object of his hatred. He said that "a thousand souls do me less harm than you do when you speak of the great mercy of the Almighty One. The greatest sinners regain confidence and return to God, and I lose everything. But what is more, you persecute me personally with that unfathomable mercy of the Almighty One." I took note of the great hatred Satan has for the Mercy of God. He does not want to acknowledge that God is good (*Diary*, 1167).

Theme of St. Faustina: "God and Souls"

God and Souls
King of Mercy, guide my soul (*Diary*, 3).

What Christ Demanded of St. Faustina

Christ required that St. Faustina assume responsibility not only for her own life but for the lives of *a multitude of souls*:

> Once, when there was adoration at the convent of the Sisters of the Holy Family, I went there in the evening with one of our sisters. As soon as I entered the chapel, the presence of God filled my soul. I prayed as I do at certain times, without saying a word. Suddenly, I saw the Lord, who said to me: **Know that if you neglect the matter of the painting of the image and the whole work of mercy, you will have to answer for a multitude of souls on the day of judgment.** After these words of Our Lord, a certain fear filled my soul, and alarm took hold of me. Try as I would, I could not calm myself. These words kept resounding in my

ears: So, I will not only have to answer for myself on the day of judgment, but also for the souls of others. These words cut deep into my heart. When I returned home, I went to the little Jesus, fell on my face before the Blessed Sacrament and said to the Lord, "I will do everything in my power, but I beg You to be always with me and to give me strength to do Your holy will; for You can do everything, while I can do nothing of myself" (*Diary*, 154).

In addition, Jesus also demanded that St. Faustina:

Tell Sinners of His Mercy

... I cannot love a soul which is stained with sin; but when it repents, there is no limit to My generosity toward it. My mercy embraces and justifies it. With My mercy, I pursue sinners along all their paths, and My Heart rejoices when they return to Me. I forget the bitterness with which they fed My Heart and rejoice at their return ... (*Diary*, 1728).

Pray for Sinners

The Lord said to me: **The loss of each soul plunges Me into mortal sadness. You** always console Me when you pray for sinners. The prayer most pleasing to Me is prayer for the conversion of sinners. Know, My daughter, that this prayer is always heard and answered (*Diary*, 1397).

Pray for the Dying

... **Pray as much as you can for the dying. By your entreaties, obtain for them trust in My mercy, because they have most need of trust, and have it the least. Be assured that the grace of eternal salvation for certain souls in their final moment depends on your prayer** ... (*Diary*, 1777).

Proclaim His Mercy

The Lord said to me: **My daughter, do not tire of proclaiming My mercy. In this way you will refresh this Heart of Mine, which burns with a flame of pity for sinners** ... (*Diary*, 1521).

Be on Watch

... **Hold firmly to this always. Be constantly on the watch, for many souls will turn back from the gates of hell and worship My mercy. But fear nothing, as I am with you. Know that of yourself you can do nothing** (*Diary*, 639).

My daughter, I want to instruct you on how you are to rescue souls through sacrifice and prayer. You will save more souls through prayer and suffering than will a missionary through his teachings and sermons alone. I want to see you as a sacrifice of living love, which only then carries weight before Me. You must be annihilated, destroyed, living as if you were dead in the most secret depths of your being. You must be destroyed in that secret depth where the human eye has never penetrated; then will I find in you a pleasing sacrifice, a holocaust full of sweetness and fragrance. And great will be your power for whomever you intercede. Outwardly, your sacrifice must look like this: silent, hidden, permeated with love, imbued with prayer ... (*Diary*, 1767).

Be Merciful

The Lord said to me: **It should be of no concern to you how anyone else acts; you are to be My living reflection, through love and mercy.** I answered, "Lord, but they often take advantage of my goodness." **That makes no difference, My daughter. That**

is no concern of yours. As for you, be always merciful toward other people, and especially toward sinners (*Diary*, 1446).

Encourage Souls That Sustain the World

At the same time, I saw a certain person [Father Sopocko] and, in part, the condition of his soul and the ordeals God was sending him. His sufferings were of the mind and in a form so acute that I pitied him and said to the Lord, "Why do You treat him like that?" And the Lord answered: **For the sake of his triple crown**. And the Lord also gave me to understand what unimaginable glory awaits the person who resembles the suffering Jesus here on earth. That person will resemble Jesus in His glory. The Heavenly Father will recognize and glorify our soul to the extent that He sees in us a resemblance to His Son. I understood that this assimilation into Jesus is granted to us while we are here on earth. I see pure and innocent souls upon whom God has exercised His justice; these souls are the victims who sustain the world and who fill up what is lacking in the Passion of Jesus. They are not many in number. I rejoice greatly that God has allowed me to know such souls (*Diary*, 604).

Write about His Mercy

My daughter, I demand that you devote all your free moments to writing about My goodness and mercy. It is your office and your assignment throughout your life to continue to make known to souls the great mercy I have for them and to exhort them to trust in My bottomless mercy (*Diary*, 1567).

Meditate on His Passion

Know, My daughter, that your silent day-to-day martyrdom in complete submission to My will ushers many souls into heaven. And when it seems to you that your suffering exceeds your strength, contemplate My wounds, and you will rise above human scorn and judgment. Meditation on My Passion will help you rise above all things (*Diary*, 1184).

Chapter Two

Ministry to the Dying

†

Death is our entrance into eternal life. Saint Faustina teaches us through her *Diary* about the promises of Jesus at the time of death to those who promulgate the Divine Mercy message and devotion. Her teaching is a needed correction to our secularized present age and an encouragement to the faithful to look forward to and long for heaven.

So, too, Mother Teresa's ministry to the dying on the streets of Calcutta stands as a monument to the transforming power of love, transforming pain into joy and death into eternal life. Among her first public works of mercy, Mother Teresa established Kalighat, the House for the Dying. Here, Mother Teresa gathered the dying from the streets of Calcutta. Here, the dying experienced love and care. Here, they could die in dignity as human beings who were loved. In these dying men and women, Mother Teresa saw Jesus in a "distressing disguise," and loved them. The following chapter (The Mystery of Suffering) reflects more on Mother Teresa's response of love and mercy to the suffering and the dying.

The lesson of St. Faustina's and St. Teresa of Calcutta's ministry to the dying is a clear teaching on the hope in store for us in eternal life. It is a response of hope to the fear of death by those who do not believe in the eternal life promised to the faithful. Death is not the end of it all — it is the beginning of it all!

Christ's Command to Pray for the Dying

In her *Diary*, St. Faustina records the Lord's command to exercise mercy:

> You Yourself command me to exercise the three degrees of mercy. The first: the act of mercy, of whatever kind. The second: the word of mercy — if I cannot carry out a work of mercy, I will assist by my words. The third: prayer — if I cannot show mercy by deeds or words, I can always do so by prayer. My prayer reaches out even there where I cannot reach out physically (*Diary*, 163).

Saint Faustina recorded many times how the Lord called her to pray for the dying and obtain mercy for them. Truly this is a great work of mercy. May these selections from the *Diary* of St. Faustina encourage you to respond with prayer for the dying, and assist you in preparing for your own glorious death.

Prayers for the Dying, as Illustrated in the *Diary*

During the night, I was suddenly awakened and knew that some soul was asking me for prayer, and that it was in much need of prayer. Briefly, but with all my soul, I asked the Lord for grace for her (*Diary*, 809).

The following afternoon, when I entered the ward, I saw someone dying, and learned that the agony had started during the night. When I verified it — it had been at the time when I had been asked for prayer. And just then, I heard a voice in my soul: **Say the Chaplet which I taught you.** I ran to fetch my rosary and knelt down by the dying person and, with all the ardor of my soul, I began to say the Chaplet. Suddenly the dying person opened her eyes and looked at me; I had not managed to finish the entire Chaplet when she died, with extraordinary peace. I fervently asked the Lord to fulfill the promise He had given me for the recitation of the Chaplet. The Lord gave me to know that the soul had been granted the grace He had promised me. That was the first soul to receive the benefit of the Lord's promise. I could feel the power of mercy envelop that soul (*Diary*, 810).

Oh, if only everyone realized how great the Lord's mercy is and how much we all need that mercy, especially at that crucial hour! (*Diary*, 811).

December 19, [1936]. This evening, I felt in my soul that a certain person had need of my prayer. Immediately, I began to pray. Suddenly, I realize interiorly and am aware of who the spirit is who is asking this of me; I pray until I feel at peace. There is great help for the dying in this Chaplet. I often pray for an intention that I have learned of interiorly. I always pray until I experience in my soul that the prayer has had its effect (*Diary*, 834).

I felt today how greatly a certain dying soul desired prayers. I prayed until I felt she had died. Oh, dying souls are in such great need of prayer! O Jesus, inspire souls to pray often for the dying (*Diary*, 1015).

Today, the Lord came to me and said: **My daughter, help Me to save souls. You will go to a dying sinner, and you will continue to recite the Chaplet, and in this way you will obtain for him trust in My mercy, for he is already in despair** (*Diary*, 1797).

Prayers for Those Who Have Died

Praying for those who have died is the practice of the Church, especially for those being purified in Purgatory. Not all those who have died are ready to enter the heavenly marriage banquet of the Lamb, because they need to complete their purification.

The purification in preparation for entrance into Heaven takes place in the fire of the Divine Love that cleanses the soul of all remaining impurities. "For our God is a consuming fire" (Heb 12:29) that burns away all impurity. The purification might also be likened to a sauna, which thoroughly cleanses with heat.

Saint Faustina had a vision of souls in Purgatory, who described their greatest suffering as their longing for God:

> ... I saw my Guardian Angel, who ordered me to follow him. In a moment I was in a misty place full of fire in which there was a great crowd of suffering souls. They were praying fervently, but to no avail, for themselves; only we can come to their aid. The flames which were burning them did not touch me at all. My Guardian Angel did not leave me for an instant. I asked these souls what their greatest suffering was. They

answered me in one voice that their greatest torment was longing for God. I saw Our Lady visiting the souls in Purgatory. The souls call her "The Star of the Sea." She brings them refreshment. I wanted to talk with them some more, but my Guardian Angel beckoned me to leave. We went out of that prison of suffering. [I heard an interior voice] which said, **My mercy does not want this, but justice demands it**. Since that time, I am in closer communion with the suffering souls (*Diary*, 20).

Our Lord asked St. Faustina to pray for souls in Purgatory on the eighth day of the Novena to the Divine Mercy:

Today bring to Me the souls who are in the prison of Purgatory, and immerse them in the abyss of My mercy. Let the torrents of My Blood cool down their scorching flames. All these souls are greatly loved by Me. They are making retribution to My justice. It is in your power to bring them relief. Draw all the indulgences from the treasury of My Church and offer them on their behalf. Oh, if you only knew the torments they suffer, you would continually offer for them the alms of the spirit and pay off their debt to My justice (*Diary*, 1226).

Chapter Three

The Mystery of Suffering

†

All of us experience suffering. Why? What is its value? The response of St. Teresa of Calcutta and St. Faustina to this great mystery serves as a guide for each of us as we, too, encounter suffering in our daily lives. We begin to recognize with the eyes of faith that suffering can have redemptive value, especially in light of Christ's sacrifice on the Cross.

Mother Teresa's Response to Suffering

Mother Teresa's response to suffering is a vibrant example of the love that the Good Samaritan (Lk 10: 25-37) showed to the suffering man beaten and dying at the side of the road. Her life is virtually described in the commentary on the Good Samaritan in the letter *The Christian Meaning of Human Suffering* by St. John Paul II. He incorporated a favorite text of Mother Teresa, "You did it to Me" (Mt 25:40):

> These words about love, about actions of love, acts linked with human suffering, enable us once more to discover at the basis of all human sufferings the same redemptive suffering of Christ. Christ said: "You did it to Me." He Himself is the one who in each individual experiences love; He Himself is

the one who receives help when this is given to every suffering person without exception. He Himself is present in this suffering person, since His salvific suffering has been opened once and for all to every human suffering. And all those who suffer have been called once and for all to become sharers "in Christ's sufferings," just as all have been called to "complete" with their own sufferings "what is lacking in Christ's afflictions." At one and the same time Christ has taught man to do good by his suffering and to do good to those who suffer. In this double aspect, He has completely revealed the meaning of suffering.

(*Christian Meaning of Human Suffering*, #30.)

Mother Teresa, as the Good Samaritan, responded to suffering with love. She responded with her whole life's mission to the thirst of Christ on the Cross for the salvation of souls. She responded by reaching out to the poorest of the poor.

She responded to the dying on the streets of Calcutta by a ministry of love that brought joy to the abandoned. When necessary, she used a wheelbarrow to bring them to a hospital or a shelter. She established a house for the dying called Kalighat, so that the dying person could experience love and personal dignity at the hour of death. In a period of five years, she received more than 8,000 of the dying, of whom 3,500 perished.

(Information taken from *Such a Vision of the Street: Mother Teresa — the Spirit and the Work,* by Eileen Eagan, Image, 1986, p. 74.)

Like Jesus, and like St. Francis of Assisi, Mother Teresa and her Missionaries of Charity reached out to the outcasts of society — the lepers. She treated them with love and medical aid using a mobile clinic. She brought joy into their lives by her love.

Mother Teresa knew well the power of suffering offered with love. United with the Passion and thirst of Jesus for souls, she made use of suffering as a source of spiritual power. She recruited sick and suffering persons to be "linked" to the work of the Missionaries of Charity. The Constitution of Co-workers named Jacqueline de Decker of Belgium as the "link" with "the sick and those unable to join in [MC] activities, so that they could become close Co-workers of an individual Sister or Brother by offering prayers and sufferings for each Sister and Brother" (ibid, p. 368).

Jacqueline had been convinced that her vocation to use her gifts in India was of the Spirit. She faced with anguish the realization that she was to live out her days far from India and to undergo repeated surgery to stave off paralysis. Eventually, the operations on her spine numbered twenty.

"I wrote to Mother Teresa," she related, "and straightaway the answer was, 'May I ask you to offer everything for me and the work?' This was in 1950. Later, she asked me to find one sick and suffering person for each young woman who came to join her in the work.

"'Why not become spiritually bound to our Society which you love so dearly. While we work in the slums, you share in the merit, the prayers, and the work with your sufferings and prayers. The work is tremendous and I need workers, it is true, but I need souls like yours to pray and suffer for the work.'"

Calling Jacqueline her sister, Mother Teresa told her that she would be a true Missionary of Charity, "in body in Belgium but in soul in India." Mother Teresa reminded her, "Our Lord must love you much to give you so great a part in His suffering. Be brave and cheerful and offer much for me — that I may bring many souls to God" — and in another letter, "You are a burning light which is being consumed for souls."

Jacqueline de Decker agreed to become spiritually bound with the Society and to find other handicapped people who would offer up their sufferings for a Missionary of Charity.

By having a "link" between each Missionary of Charity and a suffering person offering all their suffering for the missionary, Mother Teresa fulfilled the two-fold teaching of Jesus on suffering:

> At one and the same time Christ has taught man to do good by his suffering and to do good to those who suffer.
> (*Christian Meaning of Human Suffering*, John Paul II, #30.)

By doing good with suffering and to the suffering, Mother Teresa and the Missionaries of Charity — like St. Paul — are sharers in Christ's sufferings and "complete what is lacking in Christ's afflictions" (Col 1:24).

Like St. Faustina, Mother Teresa was a witness of love that transformed suffering. She would respond to comments about the extraordinary work of the Missionaries of Charity with humility. "We are doing ordinary things with extraordinary love."

Like St. Faustina, Mother Teresa saw Jesus in every poor and suffering person, and so she did to the least of them what she would do to Jesus.

Saint Faustina's Response to Suffering

The *Diary of Saint Maria Faustina Kowalska* records an extensive lesson on the meaning of suffering and its value. Her *Diary*, in a sense, is a book on "How to Suffer!" giving us her own experience of suffering and the Lord's teaching on the role of suffering.

In gathering the numerous texts dealing with suffering and then collating them into related aspects, I searched for a simple way to summarize this vast subject. I wanted to get a handle on this mystery of suffering. In the midst of collating the texts, I was inspired to use a formula by Fr. Gerry Farrell, MM:

Suffering + Love = Joy.

This equation really does summarize in a simple way the teaching of St. Faustina on suffering. We all experience some form of suffering, sickness, anxiety, pain, fears, darkness, sin; in one word: misery. And we all want joy! The missing element is the love that transforms suffering into joy. This kind of love is God's love, which is poured into our hearts. This kind of love is a gift available for the asking.

Suffering + Love = Joy

This equation for joy is described by St. Faustina a number of times and in various ways. The following excerpts from her *Diary* illustrate all three parts of the equation:

> Great love can change small things into great ones, and it is only love which lends value to our actions. And the purer our love becomes, the less there will be within us for the flames of suffering to feed upon, and the suffering will cease to be a suffering for us; it

will become a delight! By the grace of God, I have received such a disposition of heart that I am never so happy as when I suffer for Jesus, whom I love with every beat of my heart.

Once, when I was suffering greatly, I left my work and escaped to Jesus and asked Him to give me His strength. After a very short prayer I returned to my work filled with enthusiasm and joy. Then, one of the sisters [probably Sister Justine] said to me, "You must have many consolations today, Sister; you look so radiant. Surely, God is giving you no suffering, but only consolations." "You are greatly mistaken, Sister," I answered, "for it is precisely when I suffer much that my joy is greater; and when I suffer less, my joy also is less." However, that soul was letting me recognize that she does not understand what I was saying. I tried to explain to her that when we suffer much we have a great chance to show God that we love Him; but when we suffer little we have less occasion to show God our love; and when we do not suffer at all, our love is then neither great nor pure. By the grace of God, we can attain a point where suffering will become a delight to us, for love can work such things in pure souls (*Diary*, 303).

Oh, if only the suffering soul knew how it is loved by God, it would die of joy and excess of happiness! Some day, we will know the value of suffering, but then we will no longer be able to suffer. The present moment is ours (*Diary*, 963).

Each of the three parts of the equation are illustrated with selected *Diary* texts gathered under subtitles that focus on a special aspect of the equation.

Suffering

Suffering is a Mystery

I do not know how to describe all that I suffer, and what I have written thus far is merely a drop. There are moments of suffering about which I really cannot write. But there are also moments in my life when my lips are silent, and there are no words for my defense, and I submit myself completely to the will of God; then the Lord Himself defends me and makes claims on my behalf, and His demands are such that they can be noticed exteriorly. Nevertheless, when I perceive His major interventions, which manifest themselves by way of punishment, then I beg Him earnestly for mercy and forgiveness. Yet I am not always heard. The Lord acts toward me in a mysterious manner. There are

times when He Himself allows terrible sufferings, and then again there are times when
He does not let me suffer and removes
everything that might afflict my soul. These
are His ways, unfathomable and incomprehensible to us. It is for us to submit ourselves completely to His holy will. There
are mysteries that the human mind will
never fathom here on earth; eternity will
reveal them (*Diary*, 1656).

Suffering is a treasure — a true measure of love,
which reveals the true value of suffering.

Suffering is a Treasure

Suffering is the greatest treasure on
earth; it purifies the soul. In suffering, we
learn who our true friend is (*Diary*, 342).

Suffering is a Grace

... Suffering is a great grace; through
suffering the soul becomes like the Savior;
in suffering love becomes crystallized; the
greater the suffering, the purer the love
(*Diary*, 57).

Jesus Teaches St. Faustina How to Suffer

**I want to see you as a sacrifice of liv-
ing love, which only then carries weight
before Me. You must be annihilated,**

destroyed, living as if you were dead in the most secret depths of your being. You must be destroyed in that secret depth where the human eye has never penetrated; then will I find in you a pleasing sacrifice, a holocaust full of sweetness and fragrance. And great will be your power for whomever you intercede. Outwardly, your sacrifice must look like this: silent, hidden, permeated with love, imbued with prayer. I demand, My daughter that your sacrifice be pure and full of humility, that I may find pleasure in it. I will not spare My grace, that you may be able to fulfill what I demand of you.

I will now instruct you on what your holocaust shall consist of, in everyday life, so as to preserve you from illusions. You shall accept all sufferings with love. Do not be afflicted if your heart often experiences repugnance and dislike for sacrifice. All its power rests in the will, and so these contrary feelings, far from lowering the value of the sacrifice in My eyes, will enhance it ... (*Diary*, 1767).

Jesus Speaks to the Suffering Soul

Jesus: **Poor soul, I see that you suffer much and that you do not have even the** strength to converse with Me. So I will speak to you. Even though your sufferings were very great, do not lose heart or give in to despondency. But tell Me, My child, who has dared to wound your heart? Tell Me about everything, be sincere in dealing with Me, reveal all the wounds of your heart. I will heal them, and your suffering will become a source of your sanctification ... (*Diary*, 1487).

Jesus Speaks to the Sinner

Write: I am Thrice Holy, and I detest the smallest sin. I cannot love a soul which is stained with sin; but when it repents, there is no limit to My generosity toward it. My mercy embraces and justifies it. With My mercy, I pursue sinners along all their paths, and My Heart rejoices when they return to Me. I forget the bitterness with which they fed My Heart and rejoice at their return.

Tell sinners that no one shall escape My Hand; if they run away from My Merciful Heart, they will fall into My Just Hands. Tell sinners that I am always waiting for them, that I listen intently to the beating of their heart ... when will it beat for Me? Write that I am speaking to them through their remorse of conscience, through their failures and sufferings, through thunderstorms, through the voice of the Church. And if they bring all My graces to naught, I begin to be angry with them, leaving them alone and giving them what they want (*Diary*, 1728).

Jesus Asks for Suffering

February 20, [1938]. Today the Lord said to me, **I have need of your sufferings to rescue souls** ... (*Diary*, 1612).

Saint Faustina Wrote for the Consolation of the Suffering

Jesus orders me to write all this for the consolation of other souls who will often be exposed to similar sufferings (*Diary*, 1635).

Saint Faustina Desired and Yearned for Suffering

O Christ, suffering for You is the delight of my heart and my soul. Prolong my sufferings to infinity, that I may give You a proof of my love. I accept everything that Your hand will hold out to me. Your love, Jesus, is enough for me. I will glorify You in abandonment and darkness, in agony and fear, in pain and bitterness, in anguish of spirit and grief of heart. In all things may You be blessed ... (*Diary*, 1662).

Saint Faustina Suffered With Jesus

During Holy Mass, I saw the Lord Jesus nailed upon the Cross amidst great torments. A soft moan issued from His Heart. After some time, He said: **I thirst. I thirst for the salvation of souls. Help Me, My daughter, to save souls. Join your sufferings to My Passion and offer them to the Heavenly Father for sinners** (*Diary*, 1032).

Saint Faustina Suffered the Stigmata

September 25. I suffer great pain in my hands, feet, and side, the places where Jesus' body was pierced. I experience these pains particularly when I meet with a soul who is not in the state of grace. Then I pray fervently that the mercy of God will embrace that soul (*Diary*, 705).

Saint Faustina Suffered Intensely

... I spent the whole night with Jesus in Gethsemane. From my breast there escaped one continuous moan. A natural dying will be much easier, because then one is in agony and will die; while here, one is in agony, but cannot die. O Jesus, I never thought such suffering could exist. ... (*Diary*, 1558).

I often felt the Passion of the Lord Jesus in my body, although this was imperceptible [to others], and I rejoiced in it because Jesus wanted it so. But this lasted for only a short time. These sufferings set my soul afire with love for God and for immortal souls. Love endures everything, love is stronger than death, love fears nothing ... (*Diary*, 46).

Only Jesus Knew Her Suffering

O my Jesus, You alone know what persecutions I suffer, and this only because I am being faithful to You and following Your orders. You are my strength; sustain me that I may always carry out what You ask of me. Of myself I can do nothing, but when You sustain me, all difficulties are nothing for me. O my Lord, I can see very well that from the time when my soul first received the capacity to know You, my life has been a continual struggle which has become increasingly intense.

Every morning during meditation, I prepare myself for the whole day's struggle. Holy Communion assures me that I will win the victory; and so it is. I fear the day when I do not receive Holy Communion. This Bread of the Strong gives me all the strength I need to carry on my mission and the courage to do whatever the Lord asks of me. The courage and strength that are in me are not of me, but of Him who lives in me — it is the Eucharist. ... (*Diary*, 91).

Especially for Sinners

October 3, 1936. During the rosary today, I suddenly saw a ciborium with the Blessed Sacrament. The ciborium was uncovered and quite filled with hosts. From the ciborium came a voice: **These hosts have been received by souls converted through your prayer and suffering**. At this point, I felt God's presence as a child would; I felt strangely like a child (*Diary*, 709).

For the World

O my Jesus, may the last days of my exile be spent totally according to Your most holy will. I unite my sufferings, my bitterness, and my last agony itself to Your Sacred Passion; and I offer myself for the whole world to implore an abundance of God's mercy for souls, and in particular for the souls who are in our homes ... (*Diary*, 1574).

This evening, a certain young man was dying; he was suffering terribly. For his intention, I began to say the Chaplet which the Lord had taught me. I said it all, but the agony continued. I wanted to start the Litany of the Saints, but suddenly I heard the words: **Say the Chaplet**. I understood that the soul needed the special help of prayers and great mercy. And so I locked myself in my room and fell prostrate before God and begged for mercy upon that soul. Then I felt the great majesty of God and His great justice. I trembled with fear, but did not stop begging the Lord's mercy for that soul. Then I took the cross off my breast, the crucifix I had received when making my vows, and I put it on the chest of the dying man and said to the Lord, "Jesus, look on this soul with the same love with which You looked on my holocaust on the day of my perpetual vows, and by the power of the promise which You made to me in respect to the dying and those who would invoke Your mercy on them, [grant this man the grace of a happy death]." His suffering then ceased, and he died peacefully. Oh, how much we should pray for the dying! Let us take advantage of mercy while there is still time for mercy (*Diary*, 1035).

… I saw my Guardian Angel, who ordered me to follow him. In a moment I was in a misty place full of fire in which there was a great crowd of suffering souls. They were praying fervently, but to no avail, for themselves; only we can come to their aid. The flames which were burning them did not touch me at all. My Guardian Angel did not leave me for an instant. I asked these souls what their greatest suffering was. They answered me in one voice that their greatest torment was longing for God. I saw Our Lady visiting the souls in Purgatory. The souls call her "The Star of the Sea." She brings them refreshment. I wanted to talk with them some more, but my Guardian Angel beckoned me to leave. We went out of that prison of suffering. [I heard an interior voice] which said: **My mercy does not want this, but justice demands it**. Since that time, I am in closer communion with the suffering souls (*Diary*, 20).

Saint Faustina Prayed and Suffered for Her Native Poland

My beloved native land, Poland, if you only knew how many sacrifices and prayers I offer to God for you! But be watchful and give glory to God, who lifts you up and singles you out in a special way, but know how to be grateful (*Diary*, 1038).

December 16, [1936]. I have offered this day for Russia. I have offered all my sufferings and prayers for that poor country. After Holy Communion, Jesus said to me, **I cannot suffer that country any longer. Do not tie My hands, My daughter**. I understood that if it had not been for the prayers of souls that are pleasing to God, that whole nation would have already been reduced to nothingness. Oh, how I suffer for that nation which has banished God from its borders! (*Diary*, 818).

O my Jesus, despite the deep night that is all around me and the dark clouds which hide the horizon, I know that the sun never goes out. O Lord, though I cannot comprehend You and do not understand Your ways, I nonetheless trust in Your mercy. If it is Your will, Lord, that I live always in such darkness, may You be blessed. I ask You only one thing, Jesus: Do not allow me to offend You in any way. O my Jesus, You alone know the longings and the sufferings of my heart. I am glad I can suffer for You, however little. When I feel that the suffering is more than I can bear, I take refuge in the Lord in the Blessed Sacrament, and I speak to Him with profound silence (*Diary*, 73).

In Her Sufferings, St. Faustina Took Refuge in Jesus

Jesus, Friend of a lonely heart, You are my haven, You are my peace. You are my salvation, You are my serenity in moments of struggle and amidst an ocean of doubts. You are the bright ray that lights up the path of my life. You are everything to a lonely soul. You understand the soul even though it remains silent. You know our weaknesses, and like a good physician, You comfort and heal, sparing us sufferings — expert that You are (*Diary*, 247).

Saint Faustina Suffered in Silence

... Observe the rule as faithfully as you can. If someone causes you trouble, think what good you can do for the person who caused you to suffer. Do not pour out your feelings. Be silent when you are rebuked ... (*Diary*, 1760).

Saint Faustina Submitted to God's Will in Suffering

I could not even go to Holy Mass or receive Holy Communion today but, amidst the sufferings of body and soul, I kept on repeating, "May the Lord's will be done. I know that Your bounty is without limit."... (*Diary*, 1202).

Saint Faustina Suffered the Extremes of the Dark Night

Toward the end of the first year of my novitiate, darkness began to cast its shadow over my soul. I felt no consolation in prayer; I had to make a great effort to meditate; fear began to sweep over me. ... At a certain point, there came to me the very powerful impression that I am rejected by God. This terrible thought pierced my soul right through; in the midst of the suffering my soul began to experience the agony of death. I wanted to die but could not ... . That dreadful thought of being rejected by God is the actual torture suffered by the damned ... (*Diary*, 23).

Saint Faustina Makes an Oblation of Her Sufferings

During the third probation, the Lord gave me to understand that I should offer myself to Him so that He could do with me as He pleased. I was to remain standing before Him as a victim offering ... (*Diary*, 135).

Oh, how greatly I desire the glory of Your mercy — for me, bitterness and suffering! When I see the glory of Your mercy, I am immeasurably happy. Let all disgrace, humiliation, and abasement come down upon me, as long as the glory and praise of Your mercy resounds everywhere — that's all that matters (*Diary*, 1691).

Saint Faustina's suffering came from a variety of causes.

From Sisters in Community

Thus I have already been judged from all sides. There is no longer anything in me that has escaped the sisters' judgment (*Diary*, 128).

From Others

O my Jesus, You know what efforts are needed to live sincerely and unaffectedly with those from whom our nature flees, or with those who, deliberately or not, have made us suffer. Humanly speaking, this is impossible. At such times more than at others, I try to discover the Lord Jesus in such a person and for this same Jesus, I do everything for such people. In such acts, love is pure, and such practice of love gives the soul endurance and strength ... (*Diary*, 766).

... When I uncovered my soul to the priest, he was afraid to continue hearing my confession, and that caused me even greater suffering. When I see that a priest is fearful, I do not obtain any inner peace. So I have decided that only to my spiritual director will I open my soul in all matters, from the greatest to the least, and that I will follow his directions strictly (*Diary,* 653).

From the Tensions of Leaving Her Community

From early morning, the turmoil in my soul was more violent than anything I had ever experienced before. Complete abandonment by God; I felt the utter weakness that I was. Thoughts bore in upon me: Why should I leave this convent where I am loved by the sisters and superiors, where life is so tranquil; [where I am] bound by perpetual vows and carry out my duties without difficulty; why should I listen to the voice of my conscience; why follow an inspiration coming from who knows where; wouldn't it be better to carry on like all the other sisters? Perhaps the Lord's words could be stifled, not taken heed of; maybe God will not demand an account of them on the day of judgment. Where will this inner voice lead me? If I follow it, what tremendous difficulties, tribulations, and adversities are in store for me. I fear the future, and I am agonizing in the present ... (*Diary*, 496).

From Physical Sufferings

A sudden illness — a mortal suffering. It was not death, that is to say, a passing over to real life, but a taste of the sufferings of death. Although it gives us eternal life, death is dreadful. Suddenly, I felt sick, I gasped for breath, there was darkness before my eyes, my limbs grew numb — and there was a terrible suffocation. Even a moment of such suffocation is extremely long ... (*Diary*, 321).

From Inner Voices

When I left the confessional, a multitude of thoughts oppressed my soul. Why be sincere? What I have told is no sin, so I have no duty to tell it to the confessor. And again, what a relief that I do not have to heed my interior any more as long as things are all right on the outside. I do not have to pay attention to anything or to follow the inner voices that have often cost me so much humiliation ... (*Diary*, 644).

From Daily Routine

I fervently beg the Lord to strengthen my faith, so that in my drab, everyday life I will not be guided by human dispositions, but by those of the spirit. Oh, how everything drags man towards the earth! But lively faith maintains the soul in the higher regions and assigns self-love its proper place; that is to say, the lowest one (*Diary*, 210).

From the Work of Divine Mercy

On the eve of the exposition of the Image ... the confessor asked for one of the sisters to help make some wreaths. Mother Superior replied, "Sister Faustina will help." I was delighted at this ... everything was ready by seven o'clock that evening, and the Image was already hanging in its place. However, some ladies saw me standing around there, for I was more a bother than a help, and on the next day they asked the sisters what this beautiful image was and what was its significance ... . The sisters were very surprised as they knew nothing about it; they all wanted to see it and immediately they began to suspect me. They said, "Sister Faustina must certainly know all about it."

When they began asking me, I was silent, since I could not tell the truth. My silence increased their curiosity, and I was even more on my guard not to tell a lie and not to tell the truth, since I had no permission [to do so]. Then they started to show their displeasure and reproached me openly saying, "How is it that outsiders know about this and we, nothing?" Various judgments were being made about me. I suffered much for three days ... (*Diary*, 421).

In the crucible of her daily life, through the Holy Spirit, and by seeking the advice of those in authority, St. Faustina learned how to suffer.

Through the Advice of Her Confessor

"For the present, Sister, there is nothing more for you to do than accept the suffering until the time when everything will become clear; that is, all things will be resolved" ... (*Diary*, 506).

Through the Example of Her Confessor's Suffering

While he [Blessed Michael Sopocko] was celebrating Mass, I saw during the elevation the Crucified Lord Jesus, who was disengaging His right arm from the Cross, and the light which was coming from the Wound was touching his arm. This happened in the course of three Masses, and I understood that God would give him strength to carry out this work despite difficulties and opposition. This soul, who is pleasing to God, is being crucified by numerous sufferings, but I am not at all surprised, for this is how God treats those He especially loves (*Diary*, 1253).

Through the Words of the Blessed Mother

During the night, the Mother of God visited me, holding the Infant Jesus in her arms. My soul was filled with joy, and I said: "Mary, my Mother, do you know how terribly I suffer?" And the Mother of God answered me: *I know how much you suffer, but do not be afraid. I share with you your suffering, and I shall always do so ...* (*Diary*, 25).

By Invoking the Holy Spirit

... O Divine Spirit, my soul's most welcome guest,

For my part, I want to remain faithful to You;

Both in days of joy and in the agony of suffering,

I want always, O Spirit of God, to live in Your presence ... (*Diary*, 1411).

O Christ, if my soul had known, all at once, what it was going to have to suffer during its lifetime, it would have died of terror at the very sight; it would not have touched its lips to the cup of bitterness. But as it has been given to drink a drop at a time, it has emptied the cup to the very bottom ... (*Diary*, 1655).

Love That Transforms

Saint Faustina saw that suffering was not the final answer, for God's love could and did transform it, giving it meaning.

God made known to me what true love consists in and gave light to me about how, in practice, to give proof of it to Him. True love of God consists in carrying out God's will. To show God our love in what we do, all our actions, even the least, must spring from our love of God. And the Lord said to me, **My child, you please Me most by suffering. In your physical as well as your mental sufferings, My daughter, do not seek sympathy from creatures. I want the fragrance of your suffering to be pure and unadulterated. I want you to detach** yourself, not only from creatures, but also from yourself. My daughter, I want to delight in the love of your heart, a pure love, virginal, unblemished, untarnished. The more you will come to love suffering, My daughter, the purer your love for Me will be (*Diary*, 279).

Love is measured by suffering:

O my Jesus, I understand well that, just as illness is measured with a thermometer, and a high fever tells us of the seriousness of the illness, so also, in the spiritual life, suffering is the thermometer which measures the love of God in a soul (*Diary*, 774).

The Joy of Suffering With Love

In the midst of suffering, St. Faustina cries for joy. She discovers that redemptive suffering, done out of love, leads to lasting joy and happiness.

With joy and longing I have pressed my lips to the bitterness of the cup which I receive each day at Holy Mass. It is the share which Jesus has allotted to me for each moment, and I will not relinquish it to anyone. I will comfort the most sweet Eucharistic Heart continuously and will play harmonious melodies on the strings of my heart. Suffering is the most harmonious melody of all. I will assiduously search out that which will make Your Heart rejoice today! ... (*Diary*, 385).

She Was Happy to Suffer With Jesus

... After a moment, I saw the Lord, all covered with wounds; and He said to me, **Look at whom you have espoused** ... I fixed my gaze upon His sacred wounds and felt happy to suffer with Him. I suffered, and yet I did not suffer, because I felt happy to know the depth of His love, and the hour passed like a minute (*Diary*, 252).

She Burned With Love for God

I desire, O my Jesus, to suffer and burn with the flame of Your love in all the circumstances of my life. I am Yours, completely Yours, and I wish to disappear in You. O Jesus, I wish to be lost in Your divine beauty. You pursue me with Your love, O Lord; You penetrate my soul like a ray of the sun and change its darkness into Your light. I feel very vividly that I am living in You as one small spark swallowed up by the incomprehensible fire with which You burn, O inconceivable Trinity! No greater joy is to be found than that of loving God ... (*Diary*, 507).

She Was Advised by Her Spiritual Director, Blessed Fr. Sopocko, to Rejoice in Humiliations

Advice of the Rev. Dr. Sopocko: Without humility, we cannot be pleasing to God. Practice the third degree of humility; that is, not only must one refrain from explaining and defending oneself when reproached with something, but one should rejoice at the humiliation ... (*Diary*, 270).

She Found True Happiness in Humiliations

O my Jesus, nothing is better for the soul than humiliations. In contempt is the secret of happiness, when the soul recognizes that, of itself, it is only wretchedness and nothingness, and that whatever it possesses for good is a gift of God ... (*Diary*, 593).

She Freely Chose Being a Sacrificial Host

I accept joy or suffering, praise or humiliation with the same disposition. I remember that one and the other are passing. What does it matter to me what people say about me? I have long ago given up everything that concerns my person. My name is host — or sacrifice, not in words but in deeds, in the emptying of myself and in becoming like You on the Cross, O good Jesus, my Master! (*Diary*, 485).

CONCLUSION

All three of the characteristics of St. Faustina and St. Teresa of Calcutta described in Chapters One, Two, and Three are works of mercy: thirst for the salvation of souls, ministry to the dying, suffering offered in union with Jesus for souls.

Mother Teresa and the Missionaries of Charity illustrate this teaching and mission of St. Faustina. The *Diary of Saint Maria Faustina Kowalska* illuminates, in turn, the works of the Missionaries of Charity, shedding upon them the rays of mercy.

Sister Nirmala said that Mother Teresa's life was "mercy in action" (*Marian Helpers Bulletin*, Winter, 1997-1998) and John Paul II named St. Faustina "the great apostle of Divine Mercy in our time" (Mercy Sunday, April 10, 1994). These two saintly ministers of God's mercy are a challenge and encouragement to each of us to live a life of mercy and to fulfill the mandate of Jesus and of Pope John Paul II:

Be merciful as your Father is merciful.

(Lk 6:36).

Be apostles of Divine Mercy.
(John Paul II, Divine Mercy Sunday, April 23, 1995).

In the words of St. Faustina, may the theme of your life be:

God and Souls.

Join the
Association of Marian Helpers,
headquartered at the
National Shrine of The Divine Mercy,
and share in special blessings!

**An invitation from
Fr. Joseph, MIC, the director**

**Marian Helpers is an Association
of Christian faithful of
the Congregation of
Marian Fathers of
the Immaculate
Conception.**

By becoming a member,
you share in the spiritual
benefits of the daily
Masses, prayers, and good works of the Marian
priests and brothers. This is a special offer of grace
given to you by the Church through the Marians.
Please consider this opportunity to share in these
blessings, along with others whom you would wish
to join into this spiritual communion.

The Marian Fathers of the Immaculate Conception of
the Blessed Virgin Mary is a religious congregation
of nearly 500 priests and brothers around the world.

Call 1-800-462-7426 or visit marian.org

✝ DIVINE MERCY

DIVINE MERCY ART

Experience peace and increased devotion through incredible religious images from Divine Mercy Art. Divine Mercy Art contains a collection of gallery-quality canvas images in assorted sizes, framed or unframed, at affordable prices. Collection includes various Divine Mercy and Mary images.

Visit ShopMercy.org or call 1-800-462-7426

DIVINE MERCY EXPLAINED AND DIVINE MERCY IMAGE EXPLAINED

Fr. Michael E. Gaitley, MIC

Enrich your knowledge of Divine Mercy with two booklets by Fr. Michael Gaitley, MIC, author of *Consoling the Heart of Jesus, 33 Days to Merciful Love,* and *The 'One Thing' Is Three.*

Y4-DMIX   Y4-DMX

Start with *Divine Mercy Explained,* an easy-to-read, informative overview and introduction to the Divine Mercy message and devotion. Then, enjoy *The Divine Mercy Image Explained,* an engaging read that reveals hidden gems and highlights inspiring truths about the Divine Mercy Image. Together, these two engaging booklets bring depth and clarity to the message and devotion, especially the image.

ESSENTIAL DIVINE MERCY RESOURCES

DIVINE MERCY IN THE SECOND GREATEST STORY DVD SERIES: 10-part DVD series and small group study.

Now, the power and drama of Fr. Michael Gaitley's best-selling book *The Second Greatest Story Ever Told* are captured in an amazing visual presentation that will challenge and enthrall you. In 10 fast-paced and lively sessions, Fr. Gaitley connects people and events in history to a unifying vision of the splendor of God's merciful love. From the epic story of Poland's national suffering, to the events of Fatima, the revelations of St. Faustina, the heroic efforts of St. Maximilian Kolbe, and the life of St. John Paul II, the panorama of Divine Mercy is fully revealed as a transformative reality. **5-DVD SET: Y4-SGDVD**

GUIDEBOOK: Y4-SGBK   **KIT (DVD SET & GUIDEBOOK): Y4-SSET**

THE SECOND GREATEST STORY EVER TOLD

Y4-SGSBK

Fr. Michael E. Gaitley, MIC

In *The Second Greatest Story Ever Told*, best-selling author Fr. Michael Gaitley, MIC, reveals St. John Paul II's witness for our time. Building on the prophetic voices of Sts. Margaret Mary Alacoque, Thérèse of Lisieux, Maximilian Kolbe, and Faustina Kowalska, *The Second Greatest Story Ever Told* is more than a historical account of the Great Mercy Pope. This book expounds on the profound connection between Divine Mercy and Marian consecration. It serves as an inspiration for all those who desire to bear witness to the mercy of God, focused on Christ and formed by Mary. Now is the time of mercy. Now is the time to make John Paul's story your own.

ESSENTIAL DIVINE MERCY RESOURCES

EXPLAINING THE FAITH SERIES: UNDERSTANDING DIVINE MERCY

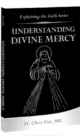

Explaining the Faith Series

UNDERSTANDING DIVINE MERCY

Fr. Chris Alar, MIC

Y4-EFBK

Pope St. John Paul II said there is nothing the world needs more than Divine Mercy, yet few people understand exactly what Divine Mercy is and why it is so critical for our times. Now there's one book that summarizes it all in an easy-to-understand way! Have you ever wondered "What exactly is Divine Mercy and who is St. Faustina?" Would you like to know how to receive the extraordinary promise Jesus offers only one day a year, on Divine Mercy Sunday? Have you ever asked, "How could a merciful God allow so much suffering in the world?" If you answered yes to any of these questions, *Understanding Divine Mercy* by Fr. Chris Alar, MIC, is for you. In this first volume of his Explaining the Faith series, Fr. Chris shares, in his engaging style, the elements of the Divine Mercy message and devotion and explains why Jesus told St. Faustina that Divine Mercy is "mankind's last hope of salvation." 184 pages.

Y4-33DGG

33 DAYS TO GREATER GLORY: A TOTAL CONSECRATION TO THE FATHER THROUGH JESUS BASED ON THE GOSPEL OF JOHN

Father Michael Gaitley, MIC, author of 33 Days to Morning Glory, one of the most popular Catholic books of the last decade, brings us his first new book in three years. *33 Days to Greater Glory* completes a trilogy of consecrations: first to Mary, then to Jesus, the Divine Mercy, and now to God, our Father. This final consecration to our Heavenly Father truly is the "greater" consecration, the one in which all others find their origin and end. 240 pages.

✝ SAINT MARIA FAUSTINA KOWALSKA

DIARY OF SAINT MARIA FAUSTINA KOWALSKA: DIVINE MERCY IN MY SOUL

LARGE PAPERBACK: Y4-NBFD
768 pages, including 24 pages of color photographs, 5 ½" x 7 ¾".

COMPACT PAPERBACK: Y4-DNBF
768 pages, including 24 pages of black and white photographs, 4" x 7".

EBOOK: Y4-EDIARY

DELUXE LEATHER-BOUND EDITION
Includes a special dedication from the Marian Fathers of the Immaculate Conception in commemoration of the first World Apostolic Congress on Mercy, gilded edges, a ribbon marker, and 20 pages of color photographs. 768 pages, 4 ⅜" x 7 ⅛".

BURGUNDY: Y4-DDBURG

FAUSTINA
THE MYSTIC AND HER MESSAGE

Follow the path of Faustina on her journey to sainthood. Award-winning author and historian Dr. Ewa Czaczkowska tenaciously pursued Faustina to ultimately produce a biography that masterfully tracks this mystic's riveting life and her unique call from Jesus. More than 70,000 copies of the original Polish edition were sold within three

Y4-BIOSF

months of its release. Now licensed for English distribution exclusively through Marian Press, *Faustina: The Mystic and Her Message* provides new details about this remarkable woman and rare photographs of her. In this biography, get to know the real Faustina, her message, and her mission. 456 pages, 32-page photo insert, 7 x 9.5 inches.